DAYS TO

Awaken the
Writer
Within

Also in the 21 Days series

21 Days to Become a Money Magnet
by Marie-Claire Carlyle

21 Days to Decode Your Dreams
by Leon Nacson

21 Days to Explore Your Past Lives
by Denise Linn

21 Days to Find Success and Inner Peace
by Dr. Wayne W. Dyer

21 Days to Master Numerology
by David A. Phillips

21 Days to Understand Qabalah
by David Wells

21 Days to Unlock the Power of Affirmations
by Louise Hay

21 Days to Work with Crystals
by Judy Hall

21
DAYS TO

Awaken the
Writer
Within

Find Joy in Creative Writing
and Discover Your Unique Voice

LISA FUGARD

HAY HOUSE

Carlsbad, California • New York City
London • Sydney • New Delhi

Published in the United Kingdom by:
Hay House UK Ltd, The Sixth Floor, Watson House,
54 Baker Street, London W1U 7BU
Tel: +44 (0)20 3927 7290; www.hayhouse.co.uk

Published in the United States of America by:
Hay House Inc., PO Box 5100, Carlsbad, CA 92018-5100
Tel: (1) 760 431 7695 or (800) 654 5126; www.hayhouse.com

Published in Australia by:
Hay House Australia Pty Ltd, 18/36 Ralph St, Alexandria NSW 2015
Tel: (61) 2 9669 4299; www.hayhouse.com.au

Published in India by:
Hay House Publishers India, Muskaan Complex,
Plot No.3, B-2, Vasant Kunj, New Delhi 110 070
Tel: (91) 11 4176 1620; www.hayhouse.co.in

A catalogue record for this book is available from the British Library.

Tradepaper ISBN: 978-1-4019-7181-6
E-book ISBN: 978-1-78180-046-1
Audiobook ISBN: 978-1-78817-859-4

10 9 8 7 6 5 4 3 2 1

Printed in the United States of America

Contents

Publisher's Note   vii

Introduction   ix

Day 1: Why Write?   1

Day 2: Establish the Habit   9

Day 3: First Drafts   15

Day 4: Keep a Notebook   23

Day 5: Delight with Words   29

Day 6: Discover Your Process   35

Day 7: Sentences   41

Day 8: The Muse   49

Day 9: The Sensory World   55

Day 10: Permission to Write Badly   61

Day 11: Write What You Know   67

Day 12: The Perfect Life for a Writer   75

Day 13: Slip into Character   83

Day 14: Plot   89

Day 15: Replenish the Well   93

Day 16: Write What You Don't Know   99

Day 17: Point of View   103

Day 18: Why Are You Leaving?   111

Day 19: More on the Craft   117

Day 20: The Process of Revision   123

Day 21: Read!   131

Afterword   135

Bibliography   139

About the Author   141

Publisher's Note

Research has shown that establishing a habit requires 21 days' practice. That's why Hay House has decided to adapt the work of some of its most prestigious authors into these short, 21-day courses, designed specifically to develop new mastery of subjects such as creative writing.

Other titles that will help you to further explore the concepts featured in the 21-day program are listed at the beginning of this book.

Introduction

I remember the morning when I sat down at the kitchen table in my basement apartment in Brooklyn, New York, with an antiquated word processor and thought to myself, *Yes, I'm going to take my writing seriously. I'm not just going to talk about it—I'm going to do it. I have stories to tell.* My table was a wooden hatch-cover from a ship that I'd bought at a flea market. The dimly lit word processor only showed three lines of text at a time and from my chair I could see the feet and the lower legs of passers by on Henry Street. I could hear dogs yapping in the grooming parlor next door. The story I was working on was called *A Little Piece of Black*, and back then my handwriting was quite legible.

Days later, a kind of panic seized me as I stared at the half-legs on the street. *Who will read it and what will I say? What if I can't do it?* And the worst one of all: *How dare I do it?* That last statement arose from the fact that I come from a family of writers and I was struggling to claim my own voice.

What I didn't know then was that I was embarking on an extraordinary journey of discovery: of characters; of my ideas and what I thought about the world; of my past and my childhood; of what I cared most deeply for. As the French writer Anaïs Nin said, "We write to taste life twice, in the moment and in retrospection."

I played with the myriad ways one can tell a story, and learned to trust my own process as a writer. Those discoveries continue each time I sit down with my pen or my laptop, and most days there is a quiet and abiding joy to be found. My wish for you is that you, too, experience that joy as we embark on these 21 days together.

DAY 1

Why Write?

Today we're going to get started by taking a look at *why* people write.

In the early months, when I was working on a short story, I read an interview with a writer who said that people should only write if they have to, if they can't imagine *not* doing it. This unsettled me. I didn't know if I emphatically had to. And if I didn't, should I even try to? I felt that I was just out of the starting gate and I was already excluded. So let's get rid of that popular belief and look at some other reasons why we *should* write.

The desire to tell stories is universal. Whether they are highly imaginative tales or stories about your passions and beliefs; stories from your life or ones that arrive unbidden: it's in your nature to tell them. So write because *you want to*. Perhaps it's as simple as that. It's the reason you're doing this 21-day course, isn't it? Maybe you are already brimming over with ideas and are looking for encouragement and support.

Write because it's a secret passageway, a door that swings open to reveal unexplored worlds. It's a companion and a balm. It will challenge you and provoke you in all the right ways. There is an essential, private relationship between you and the world that is revealed when you sit down with a blank page.

Write because it's an experience full of time travel and adventure. I once had a writing teacher who compared writers to explorers. Our job, he said, was to make trips to the frontiers—epic trips, sometimes arduous ones—and send back dispatches on what we found there. How do you interpret those frontiers? For me they are the far reaches of my experience married with my imagination. The riskier, the better, I say. For some of us those frontiers are mysterious places of heightened emotion. Make the journey and send back news.

Write because when you have fashioned that essay or that short story, tightened your prose, weeded out all that is superfluous, used your craft to the best of your ability to delight or provoke or challenge or entertain your readers, then you can step back and take pleasure in your accomplishment.

Above all, write because it gives you joy.

As you make this journey through the 21 days, this commitment to establishing the habit of writing, you will probably at times experience a whole range of emotions. You'll feel in turn elated, doubtful, curious, frustrated, and deeply content. You'll also probably consider at some point (one of my favorites): *Oh heck, who am I to even think of doing this? I feel naked and raw and far too exposed.* You're not alone. This is a place of vulnerability that all the writers I know have visited. There are riches awaiting you if you make a space for that vulnerability. When you give up all of your plans for success, when you simply settle into that place of humility, of not knowing, when you take the pressure off of yourself, the writing that unfolds will be honest and not bound up in your ego. You will taste a quiet and private joy that can bring you back to the page again and again.

Each day's reading will include exercises—or, as I like to call them, "Creative Prompts." There is no right or wrong way to do them. Just dive right in. Some of them will mine your personal experience; others will lead you into fictional terrain. Several of them will "turn the motor." That's what we're after—the moment when the passing of an hour happens in a flash, when you can't bear to tear yourself away from your work, when a story or an essay is unleashed.

Have a notebook or a pad handy as you read each day, or open a folder on your computer. Do whatever makes you feel most comfortable. From teaching many workshops I know the alchemy that occurs when a group of writers gather together to learn about the craft, to share work. They make a commitment to show up and often take unexpected and thrilling creative journeys. You're making that same commitment here, and that same alchemy is at work for you.

Creative Prompt: Capturing "Shimmering Images"

"A man's work is nothing but this long slow trek through the detours of art to discover those two or three great images when his heart first opened."

I was sitting on an airplane nearly two decades ago when I read these words by Albert Camus. I found them to be deeply mysterious and true, and flashes of the stretch of rocky coastline where I lived as a child came to mind. I love the looping journey of this quote, the way it takes me back to a time when I didn't have the language ability that I do now, back to a time when images resonated in deep and strange ways, back to a time when I couldn't always name or explain what I was feeling. Were those afternoons when I flopped down amid the yellow wildflowers with my dogs, examples of the moments Camus is describing? I know the point is not to get there but to keep exploring, to remain open. This is one of the reasons to write, to get to the heart of the matter, to get to those tender places.

When you read that quote, did a particular place or moment come to mind? Some writers call these "shimmering images," moments that are vividly alive for you and inexplicable in the way they touch you, the way they linger. Maybe you have more than one. Write a few paragraphs about each one of them. Remember the only way to do this is *your* way. Be willing *not* to know. If something else shows up—a character, another moment you suddenly want to write about—be like a scent hound and follow its trail. Trust what shows up on the page.

Creative Prompt:
Letting the Skeleton out of the Closet

I start all of my writing workshops with the following exercise and always with this odd request: *Write it on a piece of paper and then tear it up or burn it. This one is not for a notebook that you leave around.* Write a few paragraphs about something you would usually feel uncomfortable writing about. Many of us draw on personal experiences, so now I'd like you to find the one thing that you are highly resistant to revealing in case "they" (your partner, your children, your parents, your neighbors, or your best friend) might think badly of you. Maybe you fear you'd be labeled as untrustworthy or you'd be betraying someone. Write a few paragraphs about this experience, event, memory, or desire—whatever it may be. And then destroy the paper: tear it up into little pieces or burn it. There will be more about this exercise later on.

DAY 2

Establish the Habit

Today's topic is how to establish a writing habit. I'm going to begin by telling you about an experience I had when I was starting out as a writer.

"I'm like a shopkeeper," he said in a thickly accented voice. "I'm open for business from 9 'til 1." He had published several books and I sat in the hall listening intently. Like many "young" writers ("young" meaning I was fairly new to the process), the question of how to be more disciplined gnawed at me. I was passionate about the craft, afire with stories and essays I wanted to write, but I also struggled to sit down and do it. "Maybe I'll have a customer, maybe I won't," he went on. "Regardless, I show up. I do this every day. I open the shop." Taken with his analogy, his accent, and that impressive stack of books on the table beside him, I attempted to follow his example the next day. Five aching hours? I nearly went out of my mind. It was then that I realized the ability to sit, to simply be, to settle and still oneself (because that is what I do when I work) is a habit that develops over time. I'd set the bar far too high. I didn't yet have the stamina.

But let's backtrack for a moment and consider that word "discipline." This is a book about writing, after all, and the power of words. They evoke sensations, have connotations, and invite memories, while that word "discipline" whisks me back to my school days. It's mid-morning and there is gray-eyed Sister Ann intoning about algebra while through the window I watch a vervet monkey swinging through the blue gum trees. (This was a frequent occurrence, as I grew up in South Africa.) *Oh please, get me out of this classroom!*, I think. That's what discipline represents to me. I'd rather be with that monkey. When I told this to a teacher of mine, she wisely suggested I change the terminology. "Abandon 'discipline,'" she said, "and become a 'disciple.'" I liked that because it connected me back to my love of story-telling.

But still there are days when I dodge time spent with my work. Those voices that I heard in the basement apartment in Brooklyn visit occasionally. *What if I'm a fraud? What if my writing touches some tender place within? What if I have nothing to say?* They rattle me a little less, and recognizing them now as a place of nervous anticipation allows me to move beyond them and pick up my pen.

Writing does take a level of commitment. Now there's another word that might leave some of us feeling squirrelly. Take a moment and realistically assess how much time you would love to give to this 21-day course. Does sitting down each day for half an hour sound do-able to you? Forty-five minutes?

An hour? It's far better to have a goal that supports you, as opposed to saying you're going to write for two hours and then quitting after Day 8 because it's not working for you. Also, ask yourself if you do well with goals. I don't, unless life circumstances dictate them. If you're like me then take a more fluid approach and write as long as it delights you.

You can also experiment with the "container." There have been weeks when working for two or three hours feels confining to me, like a jail sentence. Then I switch it and I commit to writing 1,000 words or three pages a day. Sometimes this takes an hour, sometimes three. You could work for 45 minutes, take a 15-minute break and then come back. Regardless of how you approach this, know that as you progress as a writer your stamina will increase and soon being present with your work for two or three hours, or 1,000 or 2,000 words, won't seem so daunting.

As you spend more time writing, you may find that certain hours in the day or night are golden times. I work well in the morning, but my favorite time is from 4pm in the afternoon until around 7pm in the evening. If I can work my schedule around that time—and it doesn't always happen, as I have a young son—I have no problem sitting down. That sense of the day winding down and the approaching twilight always lead me deeper into my work.

Remember, there's a reward in showing up. The writer Franz Kafka speaks eloquently of those moments:

> *You do not need to leave your room. Remain sitting at your table and listen. Do not even listen, simply wait. Do not even wait, be quite still and solitary. The world will freely offer itself to you to be unmasked. It has no choice, it will roll in ecstasy at your feet.*

Creative Prompt: Exploring Time

The first time I...

The last time I...

These statements are ways of marking time, noting passages in our lives. They can be richly resonant, tinged with regret, or they can hold the possibility of great adventure. Sometimes there will be connections between the first time something happened and the last time. Write down five first times from your life and five last times. Don't think too much about this—just dive in. Now pick one from each list and explore it further. Dig a little deeper and see if there are any connections between one of your firsts and one of your lasts.

DAY 3

First Drafts

Ideas for stories and personal essays are everywhere: they're walking past you on the street, hidden in a five-line article on page 9 of your local newspaper, in your dreams, in a memory of your grandmother sitting in her wheelchair after Sunday lunch, in the "Don't ... don't ... I'm telling you don't ... " that the woman in the coffee shop hisses into her cell phone. But how do you get those ideas down onto paper in a first draft? That's our topic for today.

Maybe inspiration is already nudging you? Is there a question or an idea that's been niggling at you, a memory or an image from your childhood that haunts you? Set down one word, then another, and then a sentence—an elastic reach, a stretch using language to conjure that shimmering, at times illusive world in your mind's eye. This is how the work begins. And then the writer is on the trail.

If a character or a line of dialog shows up and lodges itself in your imagination, follow that character, that conversation. Say yes to the promptings; have patience and the all-important willingness "not to know." What you bring to the table as a writer is the way you *see* the world. Stick with that. Not the way you think you should, not the way you think might make money. *You*—your slant on things, your perceptions—that's the best you can offer the page.

It sounds simple and yet sometimes you will falter. Some trails will go cold; you'll pursue an idea for an article or a story for a while and then you might lose interest. There are times when fear kicks in, or lack of faith, or the perfectionist who derides the work with their commentary shows up. (There will be more about that voice and how to skillfully work with it on Day 8.) Be willing to leave imperfection in your wake. Write to the end, or what you believe is the end. Without that first draft you cannot delve into the important questions—what am I writing about, what's at stake, what are my themes? First drafts are like forays into a mine; you will unearth jewels and also a great deal of rough material. Don't fall into the trap of endlessly rewriting and refining your first paragraph. You might jettison it. Write; write to the end.

Here's the first of many contradictions and caveats in this book: This is my process, and I'm a writer who works in a mild state of disorder. This concerned me, just a tad, until a friend talked to me about Chaos Theory. I understood almost nothing of what he said, except that order came out of chaos. But I did love those two words "Chaos Theory." All my efforts at organizing myself with note cards and cork boards and neatly labeled files haven't contributed that much to my process; in fact, they've been stalling techniques. With my scattered way of working I've written short stories, a novel, travel articles, reviews, and essays. My "chaos" seems to suit me just fine and I've made peace with it.

Does that sound like you? Some of you are probably nodding, others vigorously shaking your heads in dismay, thinking *absolutely not*. If you're in the latter group then look after your need for order—up to a point. Maybe you'll write a little slower, maybe you'll ponder a while before setting words down. Be as honest with yourself as you can and if your need to have it just so is indeed a stalling technique, then dive in and get messy with your writing life.

Some writers can easily write a page or two, but then they feel stumped. They have notebooks of beginnings for stories and essays, all rich with possibility. Baffled by what happens next, overwhelmed at the notion of working on the "middle," they abandon work. If you're just starting out don't fret if this happens to you, as not every idea comes to full realization. If you've been writing for a while and are feeling frustrated because you tend to sputter out after a few pages, use this course to challenge yourself, and write into the unknown. Muddle through, stumble along into the middle and onto what you believe is the end. It's a first draft—it doesn't have to be perfect. You might even abandon pages and pages of the work, but if you don't write what you consider to be the bad ones, you probably won't write those pages deep in the work that please you either.

Creative Prompt: Starting Stories

This is one exercise to do for the duration of the course. Write down the opening sentences for five different stories. You don't have to figure out what happens next. There's no obligation here to finish anything. Let your imagination roam free. Think about starting in *media res*—that is, in the middle of a scene or unfolding event.

Creative Prompt: Discovering Journeys

You'll be going on a journey as you write your way through these 21 days. The books, the essays, the stories we read also take us on journeys. I know that's one of the reasons why I love to read. Where is the author going to take me? What will I discover about myself or about the character?

Here is a three-part exercise to help you discover journeys you might want to explore further. Reflecting on your life, jot down several sentences using the template below.

I used to… (fill in the blank), but now I'm… (fill in the blank).

For example:

I used to work in the theater, but now I'm a writer.

I used to wear flats every morning, but now I put on heels.

I used to play cards, but now I can't bear to look at them.

Then take a fictional leap and write down several sentences, using the same template for:

1. a ten-year-old girl who is an only child

2. a retired surgeon

3. a woman in her thirties who invested in a race horse

Now make up three more characters of your own and do this exercise again.

Pick two that interest you: one from your own experience and a fictional one. How did you get from there to here? How did your character do it? Surely there were obstacles you had to overcome? How did you manage it? How did the character do it? Were there times when they faltered? There's a journey in each of these themes and those journeys provide fertile ground for an essay or a story.

DAY 4

Keep a Notebook

Today I'd like to explain how important it is, as a writer, to jot down your spur-of-the-moment ideas or flashes of insight into an essay you're working on. Write them down in a notebook, on a napkin, on the back of an envelope, on the parking ticket that you still have to pay. If you don't have a pen, use eyeliner or lipstick or borrow something from a stranger. It might not be an insight at all; it might not be something you ever use again. That's not the point—*write it down.*

I recommend you carry a notebook around with you. When you use it you'll be sending a message to your innate creativity, that guileless place of innocence, to keep sending you ideas. Think of it as a shaggy, friendly dog. Out it goes, flushes out an idea and shows up, feathery tail wagging, at your side, panting, "Hey, hey … hey look what I found! You could write a children's story about Opposite Day. And then you could write an essay about you, your mother, and your grandmother, and how your mother is now your grandmother's age (at least the way you remember her), and you are now your mother's age—and time feels loopy." Sometimes these ideas won't make much sense, but write them down anyway. If you don't acknowledge these gifts, the creativity dog isn't so eager to chase down those anything-is-possible ideas. And you will be the poorer for it.

When I was deep in my first novel I carried a notebook wherever I went. Images often came to me when I was out biking and I'd stop next to the dam wall or under a tree and scribble down a note. I barely used half of them, but that didn't bother me. The act of writing down my thoughts acknowledged to my psyche that I was paying attention to my inner promptings.

These days I have a file on my laptop with hastily typed notes. Full disclosure: I just looked at my rather messy desktop and saw I apparently have several files—*Children's Stories, Poss. Essays* and the oddly named *Who Knows What?* I opened *Who Knows What?* as I remember writing down the idea, which was something about keeping secrets—fabulous and thrilling at the time. But oops, not so! I chuckled when I reread it. And that's fine with me.

Some writers use notebooks as a way of warming up. John Steinbeck's *Journey of a Novel* is a wonderful example of this. His publisher gave him a journal and it became a companion of sorts as he worked on *East of Eden*. It offers a fascinating look at a writer's process and the way Steinbeck tries out ideas, circles around the work and, like all of us, delays that moment of getting to the page. Yes—he, too, was skittish about setting down those words.

If you don't already have a notebook pick up something small that you can carry with you in your pocket or purse. Jot down those ideas, no matter what they are.

Creative Prompt: Developing Characters

Who piques your curiosity? A friend's mother? The woman who works the early shift at the coffee shop? We have so many encounters, some fleeting, some significant, with so many different people, and inevitably there will be someone who pulls you in. On some deep level you might have already started telling stories about that person. Write down three of the strongest characteristics of that person. Why do they intrigue you? Is there something about them that you question, something that you want to know more about? Now write an imaginary scene from that person's life.

Creative Prompt: Create a Back-story

Endings are also beginnings. Within any story there are paths a writer might not have chosen to follow, or might have wandered down only a little. Sometimes a writer will pick up a minor character from another book and develop them further. In Jean Rhys's *Wide Sargasso Sea* we learn the story of mad Mrs Rochester from *Jane Eyre*. Pick one of your favorite novels and experiment with writing a few paragraphs about the back-story of one of the minor characters.

DAY 5

Delight with Words

As I've written these entries I have been choosing one word after another to evoke those moments of mystery and bewilderment, and pleasure and torment (*torment*—is that too harsh? Maybe the word "frustration" is what I'm after) that we writers feel as we work. In a sense I've put many of these words on trial to see if they earn a place in the sentence. I didn't always do that. There's something about seeing your sentences in 12-point Times New Roman that can make them seem so immoveable. This is important: We have to learn to be curious, to play, to keep searching for the right phrase, so today we're exploring the writer's delight with words.

Let's look at an example. A woman in a restaurant spies an old flame. Does she stride up to him? Is she sidling, sashaying, waltzing, or marching? Or does she simply walk up to him? Think about it. Maybe it's "walk." There's something so clear and simple about that image. The verb you use can tell your readers much about her character and about the relationship. Bring in an awareness of the rhythm of your sentences (which we will cover in a few days' time) and you will be using craft to add subtlety and nuance to your writing, whether it is fiction or non-fiction.

Do you pay attention to the words you read? Do you understand them? I remember a writing workshop years ago when our instructor asked us to read a story for discussion the following week. In a scene one of the characters talked about *gutta percha* (a form of rubber). When we met again she asked us the meaning of the word. Only one person knew. The rest of us hadn't bothered to reach for the dictionary. Allowing more words into your vocabulary will feed you as writer, but a compelling narrative doesn't always depend on a heady use of language. Two novels that touched me deeply are a wonderful study in contrasts with regards to the way language is used. Here are the opening lines from Ernest Hemingway's *The Old Man and The Sea*:

> *He was an old man who fished alone in a skiff in the Gulf Stream and he had gone eighty-four days now without taking a fish. In the first forty days a boy had been with him.*

I read the Hemingway when I was 12. I can see myself in my bedroom, the Penguin paperback, the words on the page, and I recall the magnetic tug as those 27 words pulled me into the story.

Here is the opening to *Justine* by Lawrence Durrell:

> *The sea is high again today, with a thrilling flush of wind. In the midst of winter you can feel the inventions of spring. A sky of hot nude pearl until midday, crickets in sheltered places, and now the wind unpacking the great planes, ransacking the great planes ...*

What terrific verbs he uses here for the wind—*unpacking* and *ransacking*. I was 21 when I first read *Justine* and I ached at the end because I had fallen in love with the city of Alexandria in the late 1930s. This book and the four others were dispatches from the frontier about the nature of love.

Words are our clay—we model with them in our first drafts, taking those first steps in fashioning our work. When you do the creative prompts for today, go ahead and get your hands dirty. Some sentences will be inspired; some descriptions might be a touch overwrought; that's to be expected. And hooray for clichés, because we all use them and inevitably they will be there in our early drafts.

Creative Prompt: Exploring Synesthesia

Words have smells and tastes and textures and colors; that's a way for me evoke my love of language. But for some writers it's a literal experience. The Russian writer Vladimir Nabokov was a grapheme-color synesthete—someone who saw words and sounds as color. "The long 'a' of the English alphabet ... has for me the tint of weathered wood, but a French 'a' evokes polished ebony," he wrote. In one of his novels a character describes the word *loyalty* as "a golden fork in the sun."

Now it's your turn. Write down five tactile sensations associated with color. Here's an example to show you what to do: *She had painted the room a prickling blue.*

Creative Prompt: Using Adverbs

Pity the poor adverb. In workshop after workshop, writers are encouraged to ditch the adverb and search instead for the perfect verb. Yet sometimes an adverb is just what is needed. Your sister could chuckle and snigger, but doesn't she also on occasion laugh ferociously or smugly titter? Write a paragraph about one of the firsts or lasts on the list from Day 2, giving free rein to adverbs.

Creative Prompt: Discovering Verbs

Make a list of verbs: three of them for each letter of the alphabet. Be daring with your choices. For example, for A you could have "to anchor, to aggravate, to addle;" for B, "to balance, to blunder, to bedazzle."

Using Durrell's wonderful image of the wind unpacking and ransacking the planes as inspiration, take several of the verbs you listed above and boldly pair them with a subject. Perhaps doing so will lead you into ideas or stories you wish to explore further.

DAY 6

Discover Your Process

Just as every writer has their own "voice," so they also have a singular approach to the writing process. This is our topic for today.

When I was starting out I didn't know much about the creative process. After a few months of sitting at that wooden table in Brooklyn writing my first short story and watching the feet of passersby, I signed up for a visit to a writers' conference in Bennington, Vermont. This was the first of many workshops and conferences I would attend. I had my own room overlooking a meadow, a terrific instructor, and readings, workshops, and lectures to attend every day. I listened hungrily when established writers spoke of their processes. I'd read their books—now I was going to find out how they did it. I secretly wanted a method, a magic key that would unlock my creativity and guarantee me hours of effortless writing.

I soon learned there was no single way. They wrote in chairs, beds, sitting cross-legged on their kitchen counters, and sometimes even at a desk. They used index cards, fancy notebooks from France, pencils and crummy ballpoint pens, and computers. Some labored over first drafts; others spat them out in a few short weeks. One writer kept making corrections in a work already published, small changes scratched in pencil, before he did a reading one night. Some wrote every day from 9 a.m. to 12 p.m.; some wrote at night. Others worked in spurts and then took weeks off at time. Some thought about a novel-in -the-making for a year, taking copious notes and then writing in linear fashion from beginning to end. Others dived right into a work and then spent a year wading through a jumble of material. It took one year to write one book; 12 years to write another.

As you can see, when it comes to the process there is only *your* way of doing it. Much of what I write in here will be about *my* way of doing it and my observations about students I've worked with. Having said that, there are a few guidelines I can offer and one of them involves writing. Are you laughing? Oh yes, some of us have a very active saboteur and will do anything *not* to write. Strange, isn't it? But it's understandable, as well. Writing can take us to the edge of vulnerability. There's something so intimate and hopeful about sitting down with our thoughts and putting them on paper. Some of us spend a lot of time doing things for others, avoiding ourselves. When you write—well, you're right there.

If we never worried about what "they" thought, or fretted about whether sitting with that pen and pad/laptop in that coffee shop/office/bed was a worthwhile endeavor; if, instead, we listened to our own promptings, I think we would instinctively fall into our natural process, experimenting when we needed to. But most of us have moments when we compare, worry, doubt, and wonder why it's not happening fast enough. We want fame, we don't want it. And why on earth is this first draft riddled with clichés and sentences that make no sense? If you can step away from that useless position of comparing yourself to others, you will find another joy—the ongoing discovery of *your* way of writing. It's an awareness borne out of experience, knowing that there will be days of pure magic and of connections that surprise you, along with days riddled with frustration and doubt, and that each one of those days is a building block in your essay or story.

As you continue to work through these 21 days you will also come across contradictions. My life as a writer is full of them because my process is not static. It continues to evolve—as yours will. However, there are three qualities that never waver for me, and they could have made an alternative title for this book: *21 Days to Create the Habit of Being Open, Curious, and Willing Not to Know.*

Creative Prompt: Timing Your Writing

Timed writing exercises are a great way of getting away from your usual approach, of shaking things up, of being bold. Throw caution to the wind. (Wow—seeing that this is a book about writing and we will look at words and their meaning and their connotations, I have to stop and tell you that as I typed that expression I took it literally: I saw someone throwing caution to the wind. It just blew away! How can you not want to dive into language when you have a moment like that?) Set a timer for five minutes and do a writing spurt on each of the topics below. If the perfectionist shows up, give him or her a voice—write it out. I've done these and on occasion spent at least a minute writing blah, blah blah... boring... boring.... And then I arrive back in the exercise.

- Between a rock and a hard place

- Six of one, half a dozen of the other

- The sound of my mother's breathing

- The sixth sense

DAY 7

Sentences

Today we are going to take a closer look at sentences.

"Then away they flew over forests and lakes, over sea and land. Round them whistled the cold wind, the wolves howled, and the snow hissed; over them flew the black shrieking crows. But high up the moon shone large and bright, and thus Kay passed the long winter night. In the day he slept at the Snow Queen's feet."

This enchanting paragraph comes from the children's story *The Snow Queen*. I revisited it recently and was struck by the way the sentences bring about a rhythm that amplifies the scene. Doesn't that second sentence evoke the journey, the sensation of being whisked through the night? The writer chose not to break the sentence in two, but instead used a semi-colon. It's a wild and elemental winter journey. Then consider the last sentence, the brevity of it in contrast to the expansiveness of the night journey. It's almost terse. Night is magical, mysterious; in the daylight hours he's at her feet, like an animal.

The cadences of a writer's sentences, the meter, the rise and fall of their language, all of these add meaning and nuance in concert with the words the writer chooses. Readers are often not even aware of this, they're buoyed by a text, taken with the unfolding story. When you are next swept away by someone's prose, give pause and take a look at their sentences. Then get out a pencil and change some of the sentence structure. Does this bring about subtle changes to the meaning?

When it comes to your own work this can be a great area of exploration once you already have a first draft. Be bold. It's often best to do this on a printed copy. Words can turn into concrete on a screen, paragraphs become stone monoliths, and there can be a hesitancy to get in there and change structure. Do this with sentences and soon you will be shifting your paragraphs around as well. Your text is malleable—hammer away at it to bring your vision to life on the page. (And always save the earlier draft.) Like many aspects of the craft of writing, this hyper-awareness of sentences that you now have will seep in and become second nature.

Feel the rhythm in other areas of your life. Perhaps you're a runner and you can sense the rhythm in your stride. It's there in your yoga practice—note how it changes. I even sense it in the contours of the landscape around my home when I go for a ride on my mountain bike. Listen to classical music, the repetition and development of a musical theme in one of Chopin's *Nocturnes* or a fugue by Bach.

Above all, read poetry. Here's a poem by Nancy Levin from her collection *Writing for My Life*:

unbound

we may never know

how we hold

all we can

or how the light catches us

when we are out of breath

it's a sign of healing

to be feeling again

the real breakthrough

can only arise

from heartbreak

that which ails

cures

reminding us

that it's always about beginning

and then beginning again

as the waves crash me
i trust the sand
to polish my edges smooth
dissolving denial
revealing real while
courage and confidence
ignite my core

contraction and expansion
let the light stream in
and the stillness
after so much thrashing about
allows the body to wring
the sorrow out

as freedom floods
shadows may persist
know your undertow
as you alchemize the dark
and remember
that you always have
the strength to choose
how to engage

the clouds unveil the view

when you are ready to climb

now it's time to notice

the miraculous moments

in your life

as they are happening

this

is the making

of me

and we will walk

courageously

into daybreak

from the night

shining our light

together

Creative Prompt:
Evoking the Essence of an Activity

Write a paragraph about each of the following activities. It can either be from your own experience or you can write it as a fictional episode using an imagined character. As you do this exercise, play with the structure of your sentences. Experiment with them as way of evoking the essence of the physical activity.

- Walking through heavy snow

- Swimming in a fast-moving river, with the current, and then against the current

- Riding a bicycle through rush-hour traffic

- Playing the piano in a jazz band

Creative Prompt: Writing Bolder

Revisit two or three of the creative prompts you've done since starting this course. Rewrite them, being bold and experimental with your sentences. You can always return to your first drafts later on.

DAY 8

The Muse

Today we're going to explore the elusive state that all writers crave—when you're visited by the Muse. It's the perfect alignment of pen on paper, fingers on laptop, ideas tumbling out, characters who won't keep quiet; it's a shimmering vision of your book, and in a flash you make all the connections and you can barely write fast enough. It's intoxicating; it's those moments when you get out of your own way and simply write.

Sometimes you find yourself in that cocoon of inspiration, sometimes not, and so you wonder: *Can*

I summon it at will? Will the work be any good on the days when I feel crummy, when I don't feel remotely inspired?

Let's deal with first question: Can you summon it at will? Maybe not those moments of writerly intoxication, but there are steps you can take to settle into stillness, to open to that moment where, as Franz Kafka so eloquently said, "the world will roll in ecstasy at your feet." In our daily life we want to know; we want security. We ask ourselves how the job is going to pan out; if the relationship will work; and whether or not our child is happy and thriving. This desire to know all the answers right now is the antithesis of the place of receptivity we long to be in as writers. That still place is about being open and trusting; being curious, forgiving, and playful; and being willing to be surprised.

It takes a steadiness to get there. Most of us have active monkey minds, a term used in Buddhist teaching to describe the quicksilver nature of our thoughts. *Did I take the clothes out of the dryer? Tea's good—yes another cup right now! Oh, what was the name of the book I wanted to order online? Hey, I've got email.* I don't know about you, but the ping, ting, quack, beep, whoop of incoming mail tosses me right out of that place of stillness. Turn off your email and phone notifications when you write. I keep a volume of poetry on my desk so that if I am tempted to wander into cyberland (there will be more about that distraction on Day 18), I give myself the gift of a poem, such as this haiku by Basho, instead.

> *I like to wash,*
> *the dust of this world*
> *In the droplets of dew.*

I also keep a notepad on my desk and if I suddenly remember that I need to buy milk, I jot it down and settle once again into stillness. It's not about shutting out the stuff of my daily life, but rather encouraging myself to simply be. Again, this is my process. Yours will be unique to you. Maybe having music playing will bring you to that place of receptivity; maybe you will settle quite easily into it if you do yoga before you write or if you take a bike ride. What's important is to be curious about the times when you are there, and noting how you get there.

Let's get back to the question of whether the work will be any good on the days you don't feel remotely inspired. It can be. And that might lead you to ask: *Will it be good on the days I feel inspired?* It can be. How about we banish that word "good" and instead ask: *Will it be useful?* Yes, always. Many times I have revisited pages I wrote on days I deemed crummy and I've thought: *Interesting, I can use this.* Conversely I've reread pages I wrote on the so-called inspired days and thought: *Interesting, but I can't use this.*

Write to find out and discover how the challenging hour yesterday leads to the exhilarating hours today to the frustrating but then quietly satisfying hours tomorrow. That is how books and essays and stories get written—in one *useful* work session after another.

Creative Prompt: Write out Your Favorite Passage

Choose a writer who has been profoundly influential in your life. Someone whose voice—whether in poetry, or song, or literature, or a spiritual text—touches you deeply, speaks directly to you. Select one of your favorite passages and write it out by hand. Pay attention to the punctuation, to the paragraphing, to the line breaks if it's poetry. There's a kind of magic at work when your hand is following the rhythms set down by the writer. It's a strange alchemical way of learning. Do this often. It will sensitize you to language.

Of all the creative prompts in this book this is the one I hold most dear and I still recall the day I did it, carefully copying out Michael Ondaatje's words.

DAY 9

The Sensory World

How does it happen, that in a just a few sentences, a writer can pull you into a world as vivid as the one around you? Often it's because of the details. We are receiving information through our senses all the time and when a writer skillfully conjures up specific sensory details, an alchemy occurs and the dance of reading begins—your imagination, your life experience, and their words lead you deeper and deeper into brand new worlds, into places familiar to you, to memories you'd forgotten. Today we're delving into the sensory world.

There is a specificity of detail in the memoirs that you love, in the non-fiction books that have been meaningful to you. This aspect of the craft is used in all genres. It takes a stamina of sorts to produce this, a refining of the eye that sees the world as you write. I've noticed that when novice writers do short exercises focusing on details, the images they create are vivid and richly textured, oftentimes more so than when they bring in an essay or a story to my classes. Often there's also a tendency to rush—to hurtle on to the next gripping moment, the next enlightening point—instead of realizing that your readers might want to luxuriate. Or else the world will be there on the first page, the writer skillfully letting us know the essay is about an experience they had in Buenos Aires, and then gone! Some writers create lushly imagine worlds, others are sparing in their use of details. Think back on those two prose excerpts mentioned on Day 5, the Hemingway and the Durrell. It's all about specificity.

I tend to write sketchy early drafts and then much of the work of the latter ones is about creating those specific details. It's akin to weaving, draft after draft, different threads; different details are layered in to create a tapestry. Page after page I want the reader to remain in the world I'm creating, whether it's a fictional one or not. I want those characters to stay alive in the reader's imagination.

Here's something curious about working with details: the more specific they are, the more universal they become. Look at these three sentences.

1. My father drove an old car.

2. My father drove an old VW Bug.

3. My father drove a dented green VW Bug with a lumpy, beaded seat cover that supposedly relaxed his back.

By the third sentence we not only see the car, but in the description of the seat we sense, with that word "supposedly," the narrator's skepticism. We also wonder about the father and what kind of tension he carries. Those details pull us in, engage our mind's eye, and enrich the story. Because the sentence is about fathers, some personal association might be stirred up. It can be an obvious one, such as a moment of seeing your father, or something so subtle you barely register it on a conscious level. Neuroscience tells us that evocative writing not only makes us see whatever the writer has painted, but also experience it. Brain scans have shown that when a person reads an evocative description of a cup of coffee, the primary olfactory cortex lights up. Then there are some words or expressions that have been used so often—for example, clichés—that our brains barely register them. The "dark and stormy night" barely registers in the brain. But a specifically detailed description by a writer who uses metaphor can move and stir a reader.

Creative Prompt: Using Sensory Details to Build Characters

We tend to rely heavily on visuals when we write. For this exercise, take five people that you know well and write a descriptive passage about each of them using only one visual element. Use the other senses: hearing, touch, smell, and taste. Be as specific as you can.

Once you have done that, describe the clutter in each of their lives. If by chance some of those characters have successfully embraced Feng Shui and rooted out all clutter, then get into their mental clutter. Somewhere, somehow, they have some clutter. Again, use rich descriptive writing for these exercises.

Creative Prompt: Using Sensory Details to Tell a Story

Writing a travel essay or article is the most wonderful canvas on which to use those sensory details, and to hone the craft of story-telling. For this exercise, write a page or two about a trip you've made—one that was thrilling, or boring, or one where everything went wrong. Take us there—let us see, taste, smell, touch and hear that experience of yours.

———————————

DAY 10

Permission to Write Badly

You're on Day 10 of this course. Has the critic shown up yet? The one who says, "Bah! Who do you think you are to take such a course?" That grim face who peers over your shoulder and comments endlessly, judging your choice of words as unimaginative, your sentences as lackluster. Today we're going to discover some very effective ways to deal with this inner critic.

I wrestled with my inner critic for years (often she won) until an instructor encouraged me to find a more constructive use for that voice. "That's why your writing is good," she said. "You care and you will revisit sentence after sentence searching for the right word. You just need to figure out the best time to call in the critic."

First drafts—even second and third ones—are no place for that voice. While writing my novel *Skinner's Drift*, I was plagued with doubt. I was living in the country and for hours I'd sit at my desk—that same wooden ship's hatch from Brooklyn—feeling quite mute. Until one day I was in a rather black mood and I scribbled a few cuss words at the top of my page and then gouged out "PERMISSION TO WRITE BADLY!!!!" To my surprise, it worked. Suddenly freed, I felt like a kid skipping school. How glorious to be liberated from all expectations; I could write whatever I wanted to. And if I needed extra "oomph," I could embellish my permission slip: "PERMISSION TO WRITE A TRULY ROTTEN, STINKING DRAFT!!" I've navigated my way through many tricky moments with my novel and other projects using this technique.

In 1934 Dorothea Brande published a slim book that has become a classic, *Becoming a Writer*. I highly recommend it. She writes simply and beautifully and with insight about the creative process. One exercise she suggests is to get up half an hour before your usual rising time and immediately start writing. I've sometimes followed her suggestions and in that unguarded, slightly fuzzy half-awake state, my inner critic is nowhere to be seen. If you are struggling with your critical voice, try the exercise for a few days—it is fertile territory from which to work.

My perfectionist has a few quirks. If she can't see the words she can't comment on them, so sometimes I darken my screen. This creates some of the intimacy I experience when I write longhand. Yes, there will be some typos, but they are easily fixed.

She showed up after I started work on this book. I had an outline and I sat down to write Days 1 and 2, and the chatter inside my head grew louder. What will they think? How dare I? Gosh, it was all so familiar and still rather paralyzing because "PERMISSION TO WRITE BADLY" didn't seem to be working. In another moment of pique, I created a file on my laptop and called it *The Secret Book!!* In there I would be free to explore my ideas about writing; I could write whatever I wanted to, and I didn't give two hoots as to what the rest of the world thought. Guess what? I was tricking myself—I knew it, and it worked. A week or two later I read that file. Several pages of it have been reworked and are now in this book. Let me add that the revision was deeply satisfying and there were days when I put in at least six hours at a stretch. With a solid working draft in hand, I critically—and I mean that in the best sense of the word—re-examined the text, questioning the structure of a paragraph, searching for the language to bring even more clarity to an idea. Sometimes what your critical voice needs is simply a gesture of recognition.

Do you know the verses by the Vietnamese monk Thich Nhat Hahn in which he encourages one to hold one's anger like a baby? I find that to be a powerful and transforming image and I've thought about it in relationship to my inner perfectionist: she's an anxious soul if she's not delighting in picking apart sentences and refining them. Sometimes the simple gesture of placing my hand on my heart is enough to still that anxiety. Try that sometime.

Creative Prompt: Doing Your Worst

It's now time to write dreadful prose, purple prose. Go for the clichés, the clumsy sentences, the *non sequiturs*. Bring on the worst writing that you can do. It's liberating. Will it be some overwrought romance? Or a cliché-ridden fragment from a thriller? Or maybe some ponderous, deathly boring sentences from an imagined work of non-fiction. I'm serious—I want you to produce the "best" worst writing that you can do.

Creative Prompt: Taking Music as Your Inspiration

Here's the definition of a nocturne from the *Oxford Dictionary of Music*: a piece of music in which "an expressive melody in the right hand is accompanied by broken chords in the left."

Listen to one if you can. There's a lush romanticism to the ones by Chopin, and I always hear a dramatic tension in them. Then write a short piece—fiction or non-fiction—letting your intuitive understanding of the music inform your writing. This prompt is rather unstructured, it's more experimental than the others, so if it helps you, please get out that permission slip and note at the top of your page: "PERMISSION TO WRITE BADLY."

DAY 11

Write What You Know

As a writer, your life experiences have immense value, which is why today's topic is about writing what you know.

Are you familiar with what it's like to grow up in a small village where everyone knows everyone else's name? Do you know what it's like to be adopted and then years later to meet your birth mother? Let's try some seemingly more prosaic examples. Are you familiar with what it's like to take the same bus route to work for a decade? Do you know what it's like to live in a housing development where all the houses look the same? You could write an essay about any of these. You could write a story. Because I'll bet that intertwined with those "facts" is your knowledge of what it means to be vulnerable, to be obsessive, to strive.

In the above paragraph I've interpreted that saying often heard in writing workshops, "write what you know," in a more literal way. But there's another way of interpreting "write what you know," and that is to explore the emotional truths or dynamics that you know well. We've all experienced loss, moments of transformation, of staying the course, of having change thrust upon us. But maybe there is an emotional leitmotif in your life so far—some experience, some particular emotional flavor that keeps being thrust upon you, that you taste again and again. This, too, is fertile ground for a writer.

While we're talking about this, let me clarify the difference between an autobiography and a memoir, as it's a question that often comes up with non-fiction writers. An autobiography tends to focus on a person's entire life, giving an overview of the subject (which would be you, as it's your life story), whereas a memoir tends to be a more intimate work, oftentimes focusing on one aspect of your life—for example, motherhood or a particular period of time.

Some writers are not comfortable revealing the intimacies of their lives on the page and relish writing fiction. In fiction, skittish writers have a veil behind which they can disclose all their truths in a safe yet revealing way. As Virginia Woolf said, "Fiction is like a spider's web, attached ever so lightly perhaps, but still attached to life at all four corners."

Some authors work on pieces that can be called autobiographical fiction. The writer Pam Houston does this and in response to all the interviewers who ask how much of it is true, she slyly came up with the number 82 per cent. Here she talks about her process and the difference between factual truth and emotional honesty:

My books always come from events, people, and places I have experienced or at least witnessed, but I also want to be free to mold and shape those events into the most meaningful story, the emotionally truest (as opposed to the most factually accurate) story, which sometimes means merging and shifting and tweaking reality to fit whatever demands the story begins to make on the material.

Most writers have a leaning one way or the other. What matters most is that you write honestly. Are you being true to the story you want to tell? Are you digging deep and writing close to the bone, whether in a highly imagined story or in one from your personal experience? You can use this as one of your guiding principles, whether you are writing fiction or non-fiction. If it gets your heart beating a little faster, if it gives you that fluttery feeling in your belly, follow it. I call this "writing where the heat is" and I know that when this happens to me I'm onto something worth pursuing.

Creative Prompt: Reflecting on Your Life

Take some time now to reflect on your life and the themes running through it. We've all had moments of transformation, of loss, of staying the course, of change being thrust upon us. But sometimes we can sense a leitmotif in our life, a struggle or a journey that comes up time and again. This is fertile ground. For this exercise, jot down some notes, plant some seeds. Don't feel as if you have to turn it into an essay right away. Once you've identified your theme, write what you know about it—fragments, memories, sensory details. Ask a question of this experience, this dynamic. When I feel blocked or my work feels unyielding, a question always seems to loosen things up. Questions are like magnets. Set the journey in motion.

Creative Prompt: Finding Your Theme and Exploring Different Perspectives

Remember that paragraph I asked you to write on Day 1? The one I wanted you to keep private? I want you to read it again now and look for its emotional dynamic or theme. It could be betrayal, isolation, loneliness, infidelity—these are some of the themes I've heard from writers in workshops I've taught. What's yours? Capture it in one word.

Now take this "nugget" and examine it with the analytical side of your brain. Tease it apart with your rational understanding. Jot down thoughts on what you know about the inner workings of this dynamic from a psychological point of view. Consider this a type of note-taking and research. It'll also satisfy your left brain.

The next part of the assignment is to focus on the central character in this event or personal story of yours—maybe it's you, maybe it's a sibling or a friend, or your mother, or your child. Now it's time for the magic, the fictional transformation: You're going to slip into the skin of another. Write that event again, but this time change the gender of the central character or have them be either a decade or two older or a decade or two younger. For example, if your personal story was about something that happened when you were 12, rewrite it with a central character who is in their twenties or thirties. Or take on the adventure of having this event, or this story, revolve around a different gender. In both instances the nugget—your one word, the truth you are "slanting"—is your pole star and it will guide you.

This fictional character might have a different set of responses to the situation. Your story will probably surprise you, and maybe it will even change in unexpected ways. That's fine. Sometimes we can get mired in the facts: *It happened in this particular place and this is what I said and then they did this.* But this is only the *factual* truth. Telling the truth is revealing what you know and understand about an emotional dynamic, and you know a lot about your nugget in a rich, subterranean way. The fact that you were reluctant to write about it in a direct way—for example, in an essay—tells me so. And consider this: the act of remembering is creative, too.

DAY 12

The Perfect Life for a Writer

Today we explore what the perfect life for a writer might be. It's easy to say that the perfect life for a writer is *the one you're living right now*. But of course we all have our fantasies: maybe yours is a cottage by the sea with a path that leads to a small bay and hours of uninterrupted time to write; or having a housekeeper who takes care of life's more mundane matters; or a baby who sleeps right through the night. Or perhaps it's a life of readings and dinner parties where you engage in scintillating conversation. Go ahead and write down *your* fantasy. I'm still caught up with that cottage by the sea. If I had written "cottage by the ocean," the image would not have pulled me in as much. I spent my early childhood in a small village on the Indian Ocean. We rarely talked of the ocean, it was the sea—the sea of the English poetry I read as a child—and that word still evokes something quite idyllic for me. That's the power of a single word.

But I digress. Let's get back to that notion of the perfect life. Remember, life *doesn't* have to be a certain way to write. Yes, there are conditions that make it easier, such as a quiet morning when your kids are at school or a day when the phone doesn't ring. But even with the ferrying of children and the demands of a household or a business, it's possible to carve out time. Here's an excerpt from an interview with the award-winning novelist Susan Straight. She's published seven novels and one middle-grade reader, and her process will surely inspire you.

I wrote more than eighty per cent of this novel in my car: longhand, on legal pads, on the backs of discarded homework papers from my daughters (a very long packet about Lincoln), and yes, on about fifty of those magazine inserts. You have to write very small, around all the print on those things.

I tell my students—whether in college classes, prison workshops, or elementary school presentations—that anyone can write, anywhere, at any time, and I mean it. I bring my legal pads to show them...

I wrote my first novel, **Aquaboogie,** *over the course of seven years, often in a pale green, 1975 Fiat in our driveway, while my husband was working on the vehicle. He would say, "Check the brakes!" from underneath the car, and I would push down on the brake pedal, then write a few more pages in my notebook.*

After that novel was published, in 1990, I was 29, had a baby about to turn two and I was pregnant again. My life seemed so circumscribed, so parochial—I actually fantasized, as many writers do, about the writers' colony in which I would have meals delivered silently to my porch while I typed in a room where only the sound of birds would break into my concentration. But I worked on my second novel while sitting on the curb when my first daughter had finally fallen asleep in her stroller, and I had to seize the moment, right then, that half-hour.

In your busy life there are probably a few adjustments you could make and as you figure out your temperament as a writer, they'll come to you. Maybe you are one of those writers who will happily rise at 5 a.m. and work for a few hours until it's time to wake the family. Maybe you're a night writer. My experience is that when I'm well into a project it's easier for me to take that half hour in the car while my son is at karate. The work is very much alive then and I can usually connect with it quite quickly. I remind myself that all I have to do is write the draft, be it the first or third or final one, and some of the pressure I inevitably put on myself eases. I'm back to the reason to write that I mentioned on Day 1: Because it gives me joy.

Creative Prompt: Inventing Your Own World

As a writer you get to create a world. What a position of power! If you are skilled enough the reader happily goes along with you. You can create any world that you want, even ones where people fly or trees walk. This is particularly true of the opening pages of a story or a novel. This exercise asks you to write the beginning of a story in which one of the laws of nature is subverted—for example, you could write about a person who never needs to sleep or a dog that has lived to be 52 years old, and so on.

Here is what Gabriel Garcia Marquez said in a *Paris Review* interview:

At the University of Bogota, I started making new friends and acquaintances, who introduced me to contemporary writers. One night a friend lent me a book of short stories by Franz Kafka. I went back to the pension where I was staying and began to read Metamorphosis. *The first line almost knocked me off the bed. I was so surprised. The first line reads, 'As Gregor Samsa awoke that morning from uneasy dreams, he found himself transformed in his bed into a gigantic insect...' When I read that line I thought to myself: I didn't know anyone was allowed to write things like that. If I had known, I would have started writing a long time before. So I immediately started writing.*

Creative Prompt:
Writing from Conjecture

Writers often ask about how to handle the moments in a non-fiction work when they are not quite sure of the facts. Here are three openings that you can use:

It seemed...

Perhaps...

Maybe...

These words alert your reader that you are making some sort of imagined journey, that what you are now writing is conjecture and imagination. Use these openings to explore some aspect of your family history, a story about which you only have the bare bones. The details you use in your imagined story will not only illuminate something about your family history, but will also reveal something about you, the narrator.

———————————

DAY 13

Slip into Character

Flannery O'Connor, the American writer renowned for her short stories and two novels, has written excellent essays on the writer's craft. In one of them she states, "A story always involves, in a dramatic way, the mystery of personality." With all its quirks, personality is often revealed in the choices we make. Hold onto that thought as we discuss character today. Flannery also said, "If you start with a real personality, a real character, then something is bound to happen, and you don't have to know what before you begin."

So where do these characters come from? Sometimes they show up unbidden. A man, newly sober, is standing on a beach at night, unnerved by the clacking of the palms, the smell and sound of the sea, the vibrancy of this sensual world that feels brand new and uncontrollable. If you wanted to you might be able to trace his origins. Maybe it's a face you saw and then there's a story someone told you and perhaps some aspects of your nature are in there. That's not so important. What does matter is that you remain curious and enter into the relationship. If you're working on a memoir piece the characters might indeed be familiar to you—but still there's a deeper knowing to explore.

One way into a character is to examine what they truly desire and fear. Go beyond the obvious of "He needs to get to Tucson by 6 p.m.," or "My mother was afraid to tell us she had lied." Delve into them and find those desires and fears at the core. These can be powerful motivators, subterranean energies moving them through a narrative, leading them to make one choice after another, consciously or unconsciously. A compelling story is one that is propelled by a character in action.

Some writers create biographies for their characters as a way of knowing them. Experiment with this. I used this technique for one character I struggled to bring to the page. Most of the details I created seemed "made-up," an artificial construct. But there was one that felt utterly right and I used it like a tuning fork. I'd hold it up to scenes to see if they then rang true.

Consider the gestures your characters make as these are ways that they unwittingly reveal themselves. A woman who adjusts her place setting at a dinner party thrown by her husband's employer is revealing something of herself. And what if after moving her fork so, she adjusts the knife at her husband's setting? What's going on underneath the banter at the table? It's this kind of layering, this writing beneath the surface, that reveals character.

Non-fiction writers might wonder if they need to concern themselves so much with character. The answer is they do. You might not develop character to the extent that you would in a novel or a memoir, but to have this understanding of the craft is a necessity. A writer at a recent Hay House Writers' Workshop I taught had several teaching stories in her book, but they came across as dry and readers couldn't connect with the characters. When I asked her to describe the woman in the story she came up with a generic description and then she paused for a moment and mentioned the character's eyes. They were "deep-set and doubtful." That was it—a deft brushstroke of detail. And don't you like the repetition of the d's? The character came to life with her specificity and it also gave her readers a way into the story.

Creative Prompt:
Getting into Character

In this exercise you'll be slipping into the skin of an existing character. Choose someone from literature, history, a painting, or even a nursery rhyme. Write a scene or a story that reveals another side of their personality, qualities that we don't usually associate with them. Some writers make these scenes quite believable, others go for satire. Honor the character that has been created, ground the story in their life. A couple of examples from former students include a surprisingly tender Lady Macbeth or a fearful Joan of Arc. Who will you come up with?

Creative Prompt:
Inventing Gestures

This prompt builds on one from Day 9 and the text about the Sensory World. I'd now like you to invent a telling gesture for each of the five characters you listed in Day 9's second prompt.

Creative Prompt: Playing with Faces

This prompt can be rather dizzying—so hold on tight as you read and then dive in. Our faces hold the stories of our lives and you know what is said about the eyes. What if you were to take a face that you know well—for example, your father's—and then give that face your mother's eyes. Or reverse it: put your mother's face with your father's eyes. Who is that third person? It's them, but *not* them. What does this character desire, what do they fear?

DAY 14

Plot

We read to find out. In the books we find most satisfying a question is raised, or we approach them with a question. Sometimes when we come to the end of the book the questions will be answered. And sometimes the ending will provoke different questions. In a memoir or a work of fiction the plot reveals all, so today we're going to explore this vital ingredient for successful writing.

Here's an analogy that I find useful. Your plot works like a nutcracker, bearing down on your characters to finally break them open in some way, to reveal something of our shared humanity. This is simply illustrated in this well know quote from E.M. Forster: "'The king died and then the queen died' is a story. 'The king died and then queen died of grief' is a plot." What is the revealing moment of our shared humanity here? It's about the loss, the heartache. The queen, unable to cope with the death of the king, dies of grief.

You can further deepen your understanding of plot by working with the "Three Whats."

- What if... (that's your premise)

- Then what (your plot)

- So what (the emotional weight, the resonance of the narrative)

You can look at successful stories and memoirs and ask these questions of all of them. Also take time to recall the exploration we did into character and the mystery of personality yesterday.

Creative Prompt:
Applying the "Three Whats"

To deepen your awareness of plot and character in action, take an incident from your life, a turning point, a pivotal moment, and analyze it using the "three whats." One of the journeys you explored on Day 3 will work well with this exercise. Write down the premise, and then break down the moments in the plot. Write down a choice that you made and then write down what occurred because of that choice. The circumstances changed somehow, or they didn't and then you made another choice. Follow all these choices and shifting circumstances and then look at the "so what" moment.

Creative Prompt:
Finding Your Moment of Triumph

Flannery O'Connor has said that everyone who survives childhood has enough to write about for the rest of their lives. Pick an embarrassing moment from your childhood and write a sketch about it— remembering to use those details of the five senses.

Do the same for one triumphant moment, a moment of private triumph that barely anyone else registered. No running across the finish line or winning the hockey game; dig deeper—find that personal, quiet, and private moment. And if you can't find one, make one up, because as Proust said, "Creative wrong memory is a source of art."

DAY 15

Replenish the Well

Today I'd like you to take the day off. You've been writing creative prompts for 14 days now, and hopefully some of them have led to the beginnings of stories and essays that you'd like to pursue further. There are no writing assignments today. Do use your notebook if you have ideas, images, or overhear conversations to jot down—those can be so juicy. But resist sitting in the chair, at your desk, or in bed to do any "serious" writing.

I'm reminded of this quote by Goethe: "Do not hurry; do not rest." Of course, I've done both. I've worked like a fiend and frittered away hours when I could have been writing. I'm pretty certain I'll do both again—it's my human nature. I also strive for that middle ground, that place of balance where I do my work but also make sure to take time to replenish the well.

Bringing a book to completion takes a lot of hard work and it can be immensely satisfying. It's also easy to get tunnel vision when you are deep in a project, to write your way to a place of depletion. If you take a day or two, or even a few hours, away from your work, chances are you will return with greater clarity.

When I spend all day writing, I long to engage in something that doesn't involve words—something simpler than language, something more elemental. I need to cook—to chop, sauté, stir, and season. Or I need to get physical. Many writers I know have embraced the practice of yoga. I need to ride my bike. When I reread Dorothea Brande's *Becoming a*

Writer I was taken with her chapter "The Writer's Recreation," in which she suggests writers stay away from wordy activities, such as going to the theater, watching movies, reading books, or having long conversations. She says that if you limit yourself when it comes to words, you will be dying to come back to your desk and write. I've often felt that I wake up with a quota of about 3,000 words on hand. If I use them up in conversation and email, I will run short when I sit down to write. Remember, though, that this is my process. Yours will differ in ways large and small.

And yet even when you step away from your work you still sometimes sense it, it's there on the periphery of your experience as you cook a meal or catch up with a friend. You know it, but the rest of the world doesn't. Keep it private; don't talk about it too much. This is the most wonderful secret to have, this knowledge that in a few hours or the next day you will have a rendezvous with the work you love.

As you think about nourishing yourself, let me leave you with a passage from Rilke that's all about time and patience and living fully. It's about unhooking from the desire to achieve; it's about trusting one's journey and stepping into life.

Verses are not, as people imagine, simple feelings (those one has early enough)—they are experiences. For the sake of a single verse, one must see many cities, men, and things; one must know the animals; one must feel how the birds fly, and know the gesture with which the little flowers open in the morning. One must be able to think back to roads in unknown regions, to unexpected meetings and to partings one had long seen coming... and still it is not yet enough to have memories. One must be able to forget them when they are many and one must have the great patience to wait until they come again. For it is not yet the memories themselves. Not till they have turned to blood within us, to glance and gesture, nameless and

no longer to be distinguished from ourselves—
not till then can it happen that in a most rare
hour the first word of a verse arises in their
midst and goes forth from them.

Exercise: Replenishing Your Creativity

Now, instead of a creative prompt for writing, I'd like you to do something to replenish your creativity. For example, you could cook something. Or why don't you listen to a piece of music. Don't just have it on in the background or in the car as you drive, sit down and really *listen* to it.

If one of the creative prompts has led you to an idea you wish to explore further, delight in the secret of it. Carry it with you throughout the day, simply letting it float around the edges of the next 24 hours. Remember, much of the writer's process happens when you're *not* working.

DAY 16

Write What You Don't Know

This is my favorite contradiction of this 21-day program. After urging you to write what you know, today I'm going to encourage you to write what you *don't* know. Why? It has to do with that invaluable trait we talked about earlier on—curiosity.

What does writing what you don't know about imply? I believe you'll gravitate toward something that you are obviously curious about—perhaps an idea, a dynamic, a truth about your family. Whatever you don't know, you're engaged with, and your readers will go on the journey of discovery with you. Journeys make for good stories—we've already done an exercise about that, on Day 3. A writer honestly asking questions and sometimes coming up with no definitive answers makes compelling reading. It's real, it's true.

Sometimes we are no longer curious about what we know. Our thinking dulls around it. Sometimes heading into uncertainty brings forth a sharpness in our vision. Remember that writing teacher of mine who said to travel to the frontiers and bring back news? If you know what's there, it's not a frontier. Travel further. Push yourself.

Some of the most exciting moments I've had at my desk have been when I'm curious, asking questions, discovering answers and, in the best case, even more questions. As E.M. Forster says, "How can I know what I think until I see what I say? Most of the writers I know write to find out. There's a leap of faith we take each time we sit down at the desk and simply let ourselves be."

Maybe you are curious about a particular period in history. Pursue your interest in this and perhaps you'll start writing a short piece of historical fiction. Perhaps an engagement with what you don't know will be just the thing to turn on your motor. Does the act of doing research feed your creativity? Some writers thrive on it.

Creative Prompt:
Asking Questions

If your writing is blocked or an idea has fizzled out on the page, it often helps to ask questions. The more specific the question, the more curious you are, the more interesting the response you will get. Ask it and then relax—no frowning or trying to think up the answer. Trust that soon a response will wash up on the shores of your conscious mind, often when you least expect it. That's how the creative process works.

Pick three of the creative prompts from the past 15 days—ones that led nowhere or that petered out, or ones you weren't feeling too inspired about. Now get specific with those questions.

Creative Prompt: Writing with Curiosity

What don't you know? What baffles you, bewilders you? Pick something personal, something about yourself or a friend that you are very curious about, and get down a rough draft of an essay. I've mentioned essays several times because I think they are manageable—the form begs for compression of ideas, for use of language, for all the aspects of the craft we've looked at so far. Write no more than three pages. Essays are often testing grounds for ideas or themes you might want to further explore in a longer work.

DAY 17

Point of View

Today we're going to explore the role of point of view in writing.

Imagine a scene about a father who is going to be reunited with his son after 20 years. The father is waiting at the airport with his second wife and their daughter. The son is on a plane about to land. During the course of the flight he spoke of his journey to the person sitting on the seat next to him, a young Nigerian woman who is applying for asylum in the United States and has left her family behind in Nigeria. Who is going to tell this story?

This is what point of view is all about, beyond the understanding of the terms "first person," "second person," and "third person." Through which character will we process this event? Whose thoughts will be revealed to the reader? Whose fears and desires will be explored? Each one of the characters will experience the event in a different way. The daughter might notice that the son looks nothing like his father; she might mentally tick off his features one by one. The wife might register a familiar gesture her husband makes, the way he rubs his hands together when he's excited and wants to focus his attention. This reunion will mean something wholly unique to each of them; they will each interpret it through the lens of their own life experience.

Sometimes the story arrives with the character's voice or point of view. Sometimes we say, "I want to tell a story about a son who reunites with his father after a long absence." Sometimes in an early draft you find other characters and realize no, it's a more compelling tale if I tell it from the Nigerian woman's point of view.

So let's choose the father for now and experiment with the different kinds of narration, starting with the point of view of the first person, then the third person, and finally the second person.

First person

I felt like a fool, going up to the first man who looked to be in his 30s. He had Susan's eyes and I was there, hand outstretched, saying, 'Brian? Brian, it's me.'

He looked blankly at me and muttered 'Sorry, man— wrong person.' Others had gone past while he said this and I realized I was scared Brian would change his mind. I wanted to recognize him before he could change his mind. I wanted him to see something in my face that would make him think, It's all right. You can trust him.

Second person

There's no way you can rearrange your face. You feel it, fear, plastered across your smile. And all that nonchalant business at the pancake house—that well-rehearsed speech about how you will take it slow—didn't fool Mary. Or your daughter, who jerked her head up, patted your hand, and then went back to her pancake with the Mickey Mouse ears. But you? You actually believed it and told yourself you could take it or leave it, that Brian's response would not determine how you handled this reunion—until now as you watch the passengers coming down the escalator.

Third person

As they watched the plane touch down, Roy tried to conjure up a picture of his ex-wife, Susan. The boy had looked like her. People said that in restaurants, supermarkets, on the beach. And each time he'd felt jealous, a consuming meanness that said, 'He's mine. I want him.'

Oftentimes the writer makes the choice of first, second, or third person unconsciously. It's simply the way you hear the story. Some writers instinctively lean toward writing in the first person; others hear their work in the third person. It's after you have written that first draft that you look at the work and start making choices about the voice. The first person is often a more intimate voice. It also comes with blinders of a sort, as everything in your story is filtered through that character's consciousness. With the third person you have a wider field of vision. Think about a movie camera—with the first person you are only seeing through that character's eyes; with the third-person point of view you have a broader view of unfolding events. Stories written in the second person are not as common. Sometimes they can intentionally sound directive, as if the writer is giving the reader instructions. But as I've worked with the second person recently, I've seen it as a veiled first person's voice. Imagine someone telling you a tale and for whatever reason they need some distance from it.

Sometimes a writer will work on a story in the first person and then receive feedback from a trusted friend or an instructor who suggests they rewrite the story in the third person. It's not simply a matter of changing the pronouns. Let's use the analogy of the film set. You're going to reshoot the scene from another angle. Things you mention in the first-person narrative might not be there when you rewrite it in the third, but other details and moments will come to prominence.

Creative Prompt: Shooting from Different Perspectives

Choose a dramatic incident from your life, such as a childhood accident or a triumph—a family drama of some sort. List the characters involved in the episode. Now write the event from each person's point of view. Think of the analogy of the camera and shooting the scene from a different angle. Your father will notice certain details that go right past your mother. Your brother could understand and experience the situation in ways opposite to another family member.

Now choose the version of the event that intrigues you the most. Maybe you wrote the scene from your brother's point of view and you used the third person. Rewrite the scene in the first person. By doing so you will be taking a creative leap, stepping into his consciousness. Have you had any surprises with this switch?

DAY 18

Why Are You Leaving?

Our subject today is why we sometimes inexplicably sabotage our own work and succumb to distractions.

For several years I had a writing studio beneath some tall maple trees at the end of my garden. I wasn't a mom then, I had very few financial obligations and I had hours to write (sounds like that perfect writer's life, doesn't it?). In the morning I'd make a cup of tea and follow the path, past the vegetable garden, to the studio. I'd pick up my favorite pen and get to work. Often, in the middle of a scene or when the writing was going well, I'd abruptly rise from my desk and hurry outside. Sometimes it happened with barely a moment's awareness on my part, as if I were sleep-walking. There I'd be, standing next to the cherry tree. What happened? Why had I fled from my work? When I returned to the desk I'd often lost the thread of the narrative or my concentration was not as deep.

Aware that my behavior was detrimental to my work, I pinned a sign to the back of my door that read "WHY ARE YOU LEAVING?" From then on, when that baffling impulse seized me, I'd see the sign and stop, and try to understand just what was going on. I soon came to realize that I left the work because of a strange, niggling anxiety. The words on the page felt electric, I was about to dive even deeper into a scene, make connections and step further into unknown territory, and I felt strangely vulnerable and revealed. I sensed it was connected to that favorite Kafka quote of mine—the world was freely offering itself to me and this both thrilled and unsettled me. Over time I learned to stay the course. I also discovered something interesting about the dual nature of distractions—they show up both when I'm bored and also when the work is gloriously alive.

I continue to be pestered by distractions and I've come to see that my best approach is not to struggle with them. Instead, I question them. Prior to the moment of being seized by the urge to white-water raft through the internet (that's what going online feels like sometimes—a wild bouncing ride from site to site until half an hour has passed and Whoa! What happened to my commitment to working on the novel?) I usually feel quite fidgety and restless in my skin. I'm often fretting over the happenings or non-happenings on the page. Sometime simply being present with that skin-crawling feeling makes a space for it to pass. Sometimes I need to acknowledge that I'm nervous, doubting my writing abilities, the usual grab bag of worries most writers I know deal with. Sometimes I scribble down my fears on a notepad, underneath "Don't forget the birthday present" and "PAY CAR INSURANCE!"

I've heard of a writer who removed the browser from the computer that he writes on. Others don't have internet capabilities in their office. Some only log on at noon and some seem to reasonably manage their internet time. I've put my DSL box in the trunk of my car and I only taken it inside at the end of the day. Once I even gave that box of delusion (yes, I'm being a dramatic, I know) to my dad to keep for a week. I checked my email twice a day, hopping onto the free wifi connection in front of the dry cleaners after I dropped my son at school. There was a marked difference in my depth of concentration and the feeling of spaciousness in my home.

Other distractions can be the endless desire to clean, to have the perfectly ordered house, the immaculate desk. Some of this is fine and getting rid of clutter always allows the energy to move. You'll also know when you are fooling yourself because you will have the sometimes painful awareness that you dodged those hours that you planned to spend writing and "wasted" them doing something else.

Creative Prompt: Story-telling Through Three Pieces

This prompt will encourage a different kind of story-telling. It's a story that is revealed by an accrual of details, so that the three pieces together tell a story that is greater than its parts.

Make a list of five objects that you find particularly meaningful for their beauty, for what they evoke in you, for the delight of the words. For example, the first one that comes to my mind is small gray vase with a dolphin carved on it. Trust your instincts with this exercise. As with all of them, there is no right or wrong way of doing it.

Then look at the five objects and pick the one that you find most intriguing. Write three short pieces, featuring three different characters, in which the object features in some way. For example, a fictional character could handle it on one scene; it could be in the background in another scene; and perhaps it could be broken in the third scene. Each vignette need not be more than a page, as these are short, impressionistic pieces.

If you wrote this as a purely fictional exercise, I'd now like you to move closer to the personal. Go ahead and use your family as characters. This is a draft of an exercise, nothing is written in stone. Do you delight in stepping into their shoes (and they don't even know it)? Invent, experiment, and explore.

DAY 19

More on the Craft

Craft is the quiet delight: It's the cup of tea to your champagne burst of inspiration. What do you think about that? Tea and champagne—is that image too coy? Maybe. But as I write I like to play with language and images. In a subsequent draft I might cut that sentence. Then I would read Day 19 out loud and see if I missed it. This questioning, this holding up of an earlier draft and examining whether it is the best way to tell your story, is craft in action.

I have faith in the writer's craft. In every workshop I've taught I've witnessed the huge strides a writer can make as they understand how malleable language can be. The more a writer understands and experiments with all the tools in his toolbox, the more skilled that writer becomes.

When I first started writing I told my stories and essays on instinct. I'd write a draft, love it or dislike it, and have no clue as to what else to do with it. The words seemed to turn to concrete on the printed page. Immoveable. I enrolled in writing workshops and learned about the craft, about point of view, about inner narration, about dialogue, about working with a sense of place. I learned that these aspects of the craft worked together like an intricate and synchronized piece of machinery, and in one paragraph I could be working with place and character and also indirect speech.

At first I felt awkward, aware of too much, and I longed to get back to that beginner's mindset where I simply told my stories. But spending time with the page or the laptop allowed those ideas of the craft to settle, to become more ingrained. The same will happen to you. The craft will sink into your writing so you are barely aware you are using it—until the day when you come across a problem in your work and you find you have the resources, the conscious awareness, to step in and rework, refashion.

You can learn about the craft by finding writing workshops in your area. Those taught as university extension programs often have very good instructors. In many of these workshops you will have a chance to comment on your colleagues' work—the more seriously you take this task, the more you will help yourself as a writer. One day you will need your discerning eye as you settle down to take on a rewrite.

Creative Prompt:
Using Props for Inspiration

Think back to your childhood home and make a list of some of the items in it—items that resonate with you in some way. You could call these items "props"—props that mattered to you. Make a list of five props you wish you still had. Now reduce them to the one item—perhaps a vase, a tablecloth, a pair of shoes, a dress, a mirror—that you wish you still had. Write a few paragraphs on why that prop resonates with you.

Creative Prompt:
Writing a Character's Journal

Write a journal for one of the characters from Day 9, or any other character that has arrived since you've begun this course. Pick someone whom you feel quite strongly about. The simple fact of saying this is a journal will trigger revelations. What do you put in a journal but observations, hopes, fears, and dreams that are private. Guess what? Your characters will do the same. This exercise also touches on another way of telling a story. Do the exercise again for one of the characters who has not come "alive" for you, a character who seems flat on the page. Does giving them a voice in this way deepen your engagement with them?

DAY 20

The Process
of Revision

We're coming to the end of our 21 days and amongst
the creative prompts that you have worked on, I'm
sure there are a few you would like to revisit and
develop further. The process of revision can be a
bit baffling to some "young" writers, so let's spend
today looking at this.

I, too, used to feel a bit perplexed by making revisions
and sometimes even despairing as I encountered
problems in the work: characters who seemed so
flat on the page or the structure of an essay just not

working. Then an artist friend of mine shared some of her work philosophy with me. "Problems," she said, "are an opportunity for creative solutions."

So let's get back to the process of revision. Some writers write very sketchy first drafts and so their subsequent drafts (and there might be several of them) involve opening up the work, fleshing it out. Others spill everything onto the page, produce voluminous drafts and then are ruthless as they prune. Yet other writers, especially those who mull over their work before setting it down, have a nicely developed first draft. It's early in your process but you have probably identified yourself with one of these types.

Whichever approach to writing you identify with, it's important to take a break from your work and put it aside for a few days or even weeks. When you reread it you will then experience it anew and see the whole work in a fresh way. Have a notepad handy and write down any thoughts you have about the text—about connections, moments that make no sense, moments that can be opened up, and any questions that may arise.

Here are a few questions to ask yourself as you start your revisions (note I used the plural—revisions!):

- Do the opening paragraphs capture the reader's attention? Sometimes a story, an essay, or a full-length work can meander along for several paragraphs or even pages before landing somewhere dynamic. Make sure your opening pages aren't a form of "throat clearing." Sometimes the story begins on page 3. This is often clear when you read it after putting it aside for some time. Trust your instincts.

- After reading the opening chapter of a novel or a memoir we need to have a sense of the major conflict in the work, the setting, the main character, and the themes of the work.

- Make a list of the many failings that all of us have in our early drafts: clichés; overwrought prose; abrupt changes of point of view; meaningless dialog; needless detail; use of the passive voice; lengthy scenes that are obviously fillers and can be summarized or cut; and sections of narration that would be far more powerful if dramatized. Now reread your chapters on the hunt for any of these inevitable blunders.

- Does your dialog advance your narrative and reveal character? Do your characters all sound the same? Do they use the same expressions?

- Think about your narrative, your plot. Is it arising out of character, is it character in action? Is the struggle worth the story?

- Are your characters "wanting" and "needing?" Are they pursuing those wants and needs either consciously or unconsciously? And do your characters have choices and ways of acting or not acting?

- Would your narrative be stronger if you changed the point of view?

- Do your scenes matter? They must have either narrative, emotional, or thematic significance.

- Look out for redundant expressions, such as: "I thought to myself." "I blinked my eyes." "I came to a complete stop."

- Look at your dialog tags. For example: "'Oh, please, please don't read the letter now,' she said beseechingly." The use of "please, please" in your dialog reveals a great deal about your character's emotional state. It's cleaner and simpler if you write: "'Oh, please, please don't read the letter now,' she said."

- Look at your paragraphs. Are they all the same length? Is that your writer's habit, a tic of sorts, or is it intentional?

- Look at your sentences. Are they varied? Are you using rhythm to advance and support your narrative?

- Look at your verbs. We have such dynamic verbs in the English language. Use them!

This step is key: set aside some time and read your work out loud, chapter by chapter. If you are stumbling over a sentence, chances are your reader will as well. Do you need to catch a breath? Look at your punctuation. Do you have run-on sentences that make no sense? You'll discover them as you read out loud.

Remember that as you develop as a writer, as you learn about the craft, you will have more resources to draw on, greater skill when it comes to getting that idea, that story, that moment in time onto the page. And still you will have to give up those notions of perfection. It always falls short—what we hold in our imagination never quite translates exactly onto the page. But then your reader comes along and brings their own imagination, their own life experience to your words and in a sense they create something with your text. And so the dance begins again.

Creative Prompt: Revising a Piece of Non-fiction

For this exercise I'd like you to take one of the non-fiction pieces you wrote on one of the earlier days, and revise it. Reflect on the days that focused on craft: words, sentences, character, and the section on details, and have that inform how you rewrite it. If you tended to write pages and pages, you might want to experiment and give yourself a container of 1,000 words for the rewrite. There is a kind of freedom to be found in restraint. How economical and vibrant will your sentences be? Is every word, every sentence working for you, earning its place in your essay? Let that astute critical eye of yours get to work and see how satisfying this can be, all the while reminding yourself that this is simply the next draft.

Creative Prompt:
Revising a Piece of Fiction

Now would be a good time to revise one of your fictional pieces, focusing on your plot, making sure it is arriving out of a character in action. Look at the ways your characters unwittingly reveal themselves through their gestures. What is the setting for your story? One way to reveal place is to have your character interact with the environment, to have some kind of response to it.

DAY 21

Read!

You probably haven't realized it, but this is the first time in this course that I have used an exclamation mark with the title of the topic. I once had an editor who wasn't a fan of exclamation marks. She'd rather the writer use language with vigor to evoke a sense of urgency or enthusiasm. Her comments struck a cord and, apart from Facebook posts and the occasional email, I tend to shy away from exclamation marks. But not here. Reading, our subject for today, is *that* important!

I'm often surprised when people who want to write, don't read. Read, and read widely—and outside your genre. You will learn so much about the craft and open yourself to new ideas. Reading will nourish you and inspire you. On finishing this 21-day course you will read with a new awareness. You will read like a writer. You may find yourself asking, How did the author accomplish that? How, in just two sentences, did she whisk me off to another world? Slow down there, study that paragraph. Look at the choice of words, at the structure of the sentences. You know something about this aspect of the craft from working with the Creative Prompts. Articulating why or what the writer did will help you when you are at your desk, telling your story.

Keep the books you love, the ones that you admire, together on a shelf. It's your medicine chest—you can reach for one of them as a prescription if you are struggling with your own work. If you are having trouble bringing your characters fully and vividly to life, pick up a book by an author you admire and read, to be inspired and with an eye to see exactly how they did it. There's always an element that one can't fathom—the writer's alchemy— but maybe you will see that they used details in a certain way; perhaps the characters' gestures reveal an inner tension. Maybe their desire is all in their unselfconscious gestures and in contradiction with their dialog.

I recently felt frustrated with linear story-telling, I wanted to rely less on a plot moving from A to B to C, and more on a mosaic way of story-telling so I reached for the novels on my shelf that had been successful in doing just that. I asked questions and tried to understand how they did it. The "prescription" helped in that it gave me confidence to try a new tack.

Read because it's good for the soul. We all instinctively know that, don't we? And now neuroscience is proving it. When we read an emotional exchange between two characters, it stimulates the brain and can even change how we react in real life. And doesn't this spur you on to learn even more about the craft, so that your work will resonate with readers in even deeper ways?

Creative Prompt:
Taking a Look at Happiness

Happy families are all alike; every unhappy family is unhappy in its own way.

The quotation above is the opening line of *Anna Karenina* by Leo Tolstoy. For the purpose of this exercise we're going to examine happiness. It's so easy, in just a few sentences, to conjure up loads of clichés about this subject. Is it because the word "happiness" is too general? Or maybe we think about it in general terms. Which happy families do you know? Is yours one? List a few of them and write about their happiness in specific ways. Move beyond the cliché, don't mention the words "happiness" or "happy" and limit the number of smiles you give your characters. Smiles are too easy. Also stay away from characters sighing. By doing this exercise you will refine your eye.

Afterword

You have a unique writer's voice. No one writes quite like you. No one can tell your stories. Your voice is still young, but as you continue to write, as you learn more about the craft, your voice will develop. This is not a process that happens overnight. Time and time again I have worked with writers and seen their writing develop, seen the moment when suddenly they are expressing themselves with an acquired confidence.

As you go on writing, give up the habit of labeling days as good ones or bad ones. They are all useful. Let this quote from Martha Graham inspire you:

There is a vitality, a life force, a quickening that is translated through you into action, and because there is only one of you in all time, this expression is unique. If you block it, it will never exist through any other medium and will be lost. The world will not have it. It is not your business to determine how good it is; nor how valuable it is; nor how it compares with other expressions. It is your business to keep it yours, clearly and directly, to keep the channel open. You do not even have to believe in yourself and your work. You have to keep open and aware directly to the urges that motivate you. Keep the channel open. No artist is pleased. There is no satisfaction, whatever, at any time. There is only a queer divine dissatisfaction; a blessed unrest that keeps us marching and makes us more alive than the others.

MARTHA GRAHAM TO AGNES DE MILLE

Wishing you every success with your writing—keep expressing that unique voice!

Bibliography

p.5: Camus, Albert. *Lyrical and Critical Essays*. Vintage Books, 1970

p.13: Kafka, Franz. *The Zürau Aphorisms*. Harvill Secker, 2014

p.31: Hemingway, Ernest. *The Old Man and The Sea*. Scribner, 1995

p.32: Durrell, Lawrence. *Justine*. Faber & Faber, 1957

p.41: Andersen, Hans Christian. *The Snow Queen*, 1844

p.44: Nancy Levin, 'Unbound', from *Writing for My Life*, 2012

p.90, p.100: Forster, E.M. *Aspects of the Novel*, 1927

p.96: Rilke, Rainer Maria. *The Notebooks of Malte Laurids Brigge*, 1910

p.134: Tolstoy, Leo. *Anna Karenina*, 1878

About the Author

Lisa Fugard is a writer and freelance editor from South Africa. Her novel *Skinner's Drift* was runner-up for the Dayton Literary Peace Prize. Her work has been published in *Story*, *Outside*, and *The New York Times*.

www.lisafugard.com

Notes

Notes

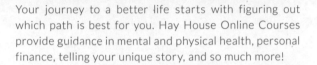

Hay House Podcasts

Bring Fresh, Free Inspiration Each Week!

Hay House proudly offers a selection of life-changing audio content via our most popular podcasts!

Hay House Meditations Podcast

Features your favorite Hay House authors guiding you through meditations designed to help you relax and rejuvenate. Take their words into your soul and cruise through the week!

Dr. Wayne W. Dyer Podcast

Discover the timeless wisdom of Dr. Wayne W. Dyer, world-renowned spiritual teacher and affectionately known as "the father of motivation." Each week brings some of the best selections from the 10-year span of Dr. Dyer's talk show on Hay House Radio.

Hay House Podcast

Enjoy a selection of insightful and inspiring lectures from Hay House Live events, listen to some of the best moments from previous Hay House Radio episodes, and tune in for exclusive interviews and behind-the-scenes audio segments featuring leading experts in the fields of alternative health, self-development, intuitive medicine, success, and more! Get motivated to live your best life possible by subscribing to the free Hay House Podcast.

Listen on Apple Podcasts

Find Hay House podcasts on iTunes, or visit
www.HayHouse.com/podcasts for more info.

CONNECT WITH
HAY HOUSE
ONLINE

🌐 hayhouse.co.uk   **f** @hayhouse

📷 @hayhouseuk   🐦 @hayhouseuk

▶ @hayhouseuk   ♪ @hayhouseuk

Find out all about our latest books & card decks • Be the first to know about exclusive discounts • Interact with our authors in live broadcasts • Celebrate the cycle of the seasons with us • Watch free videos from your favourite authors • Connect with like-minded souls

'The gateways to wisdom and knowledge are always open.'

Louise Hay